# A Day in the Life: Sea Animals

# Seal

Louise Spilsbury

**www.raintreepublishers.co.uk**
Visit our website to find out
more information about
Raintree books.

**To order:**
☎ Phone 0845 6044371
▤ Fax +44 (0) 1865 312263
▥ Email myorders@raintreepublishers.co.uk

Customers from outside the UK please telephone +44 1865 312262

Raintree is an imprint of Capstone Global Library Limited,
a company incorporated in England and Wales having
its registered office at 7 Pilgrim Street, London, EC4V 6LB
– Registered company number: 6695582

Text © Capstone Global Library Limited 2011
First published in hardback in 2011
First published in paperback in 2012
The moral rights of the proprietor have been asserted.

Edited by Sian Smith, Nancy Dickmann, and Rebecca Rissman
Designed by Joanna Hinton-Malivoire
Picture research by Mica Brancic
Production by Victoria Fitzgerald
Originated by Capstone Global Library Ltd
Printed in China

ISBN 978 1 4062 1704 9 (hardback)
14 13 12 11 10
10 9 8 7 6 5 4 3 2 1

ISBN 978 1 4062 1888 6 (paperback)
15 14 13 12
10 9 8 7 6 5 4 3 2

**British Library Cataloguing in Publication Data**
Spilsbury, Louise.
  Seal. -- (A day in the life. Sea animals)
  1. Seals (Animals)--Pictorial works--Juvenile literature.
  I. Title II. Series
  599.7'9-dc22

**Acknowledgements**
We would like to thank the following for permission to
reproduce photographs: Alamy p.12 (© Kim Westerskov);
Corbis pp.14 (© Rick Price), 22 (© Galen Rowell); FLPA pp.15,
17, 19, 23: whiskers (Minden Pictures/Norbert Wu), 16
(Winfried Wisniewski), 20 (Sunset ), 21 (Minden Pictures/Ingo
Arndt); Getty Images pp.7, 23: flipper (The Image Bank/
Frank Krahmer), 13 (The Image Bank/Daisy Gilardini), 18,
23: breathe (The Image Bank/Doug Allan); Photolibrary pp.4,
23: coast (Juniors Bildarchiv), 5, 23: Antarctica (Imagestate/
Ethel Davies), 6, 23: blubber (Animals Animals/Bradley W
Stahl), 8 (Picture Press/Thorsten Milse), 9, 23: pup (Oxford
Scientific Films (OSF)/David Tipling), 10 (Oxford Scientific
Films (OSF)/Doug Allan), 11 (Oxford Scientific Films (OSF)/
Rick Price).

Cover photograph of a Seal taken in Lincolnshire, England
reproduced with permission of Corbis (Design Pics/© John
Short). Back cover photograph of a flipper reproduced with
permission of Getty Images (The Image Bank/Frank Krahmer).
Back cover photograph of whiskers reproduced with permission
of Getty Images (The Image Bank/Doug Allan).

We would like to thank Michael Bright for his invaluable help
in the preparation of this book.

Every effort has been made to contact copyright holders
of material reproduced in this book. Any omissions will
be rectified in subsequent printings if notice is given to the
publisher.

All the Internet addresses (URLs) given in this book were valid
at the time of going to press. However, due to the dynamic
nature of the Internet, some addresses may have changed, or
sites may have changed or ceased to exist since publication.
While the author and publisher regret any inconvenience this
may cause readers, no responsibility for any such changes can
be accepted by either the author or the publisher.

# Contents

Some words are shown in bold, **like this**.
You can find them in the glossary on page 23.

# What is a seal?

elephant seals

A seal is an animal that mainly lives in the ocean.

There are many different types of seal.

Weddell seal

Seals live around **coasts** all over the world.

Weddell seals are large seals that mainly live in the icy waters of **Antarctica**.

# What do seals look like?

Weddell seals have black, grey, and white fur that turns brown as they get older.

They have a thick layer of **blubber** under their skin to keep them warm.

flipper

Seals' bodies are long and smooth to help them swim quickly.

They have two front **flippers** and two back flippers and a short tail.

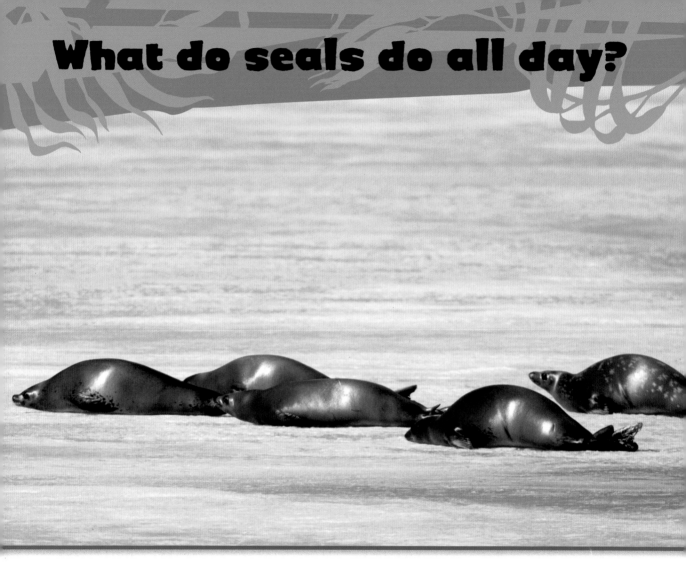

In summer, Weddell seals spend a lot of time on the ice.

They pull themselves along on their bellies using their front **flippers**.

They rest and clean their fur with their claws.

Weddell seals can rest in the same place for hours.

# What do seals do at night?

On summer nights, Weddell seals mainly hunt for food.

They dive through holes in the ice and swim down deep in the ocean.

It is light all day and all night in **Antarctica** in summer.

Weddell seals can see fish as the light shines through the ice.

# What do seals eat?

Weddell seals catch and eat their food in the water.

They mainly eat fish and other small sea animals.

teeth

Seals have sharp teeth and claws for holding food.

They swallow fish whole or in big chunks.

# How do seals find food?

Before seals dive, they close their nostrils and mouth.

They can stay underwater for about 20 minutes.

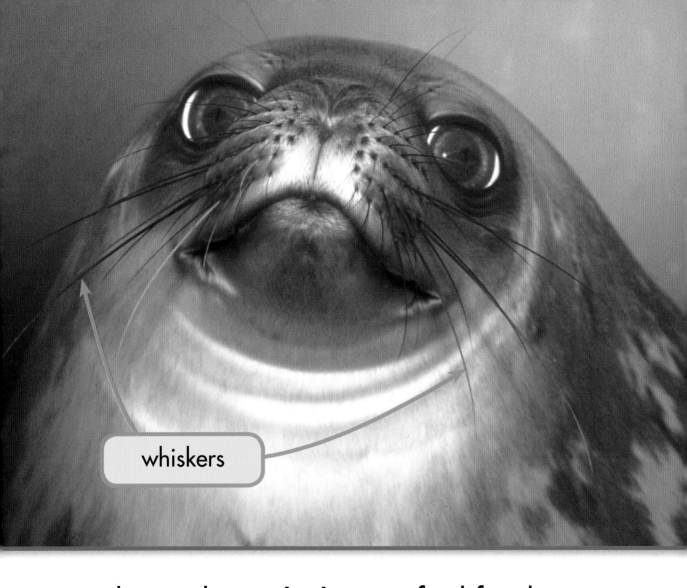

whiskers

Seals use their **whiskers** to find food in deep and dark water.

Seals can feel where fish are moving with their whiskers.

# What are seal babies like?

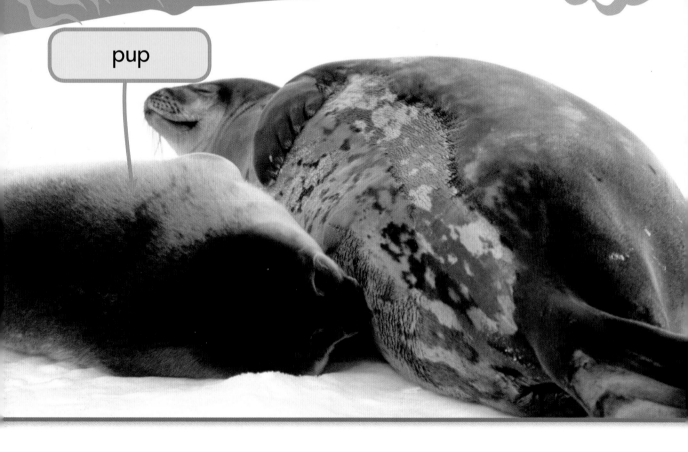

pup

Seal babies are called **pups**.

A Weddell seal pup has soft grey, brown, or golden fur.

Pups feed on milk from their mother's body.

They follow their mothers to learn how to swim, dive, and hunt.

# What do seals do in winter?

In winter, Weddell seals live and feed under the ice all the time.

They chew at the ice with their teeth to make holes to **breathe** through.

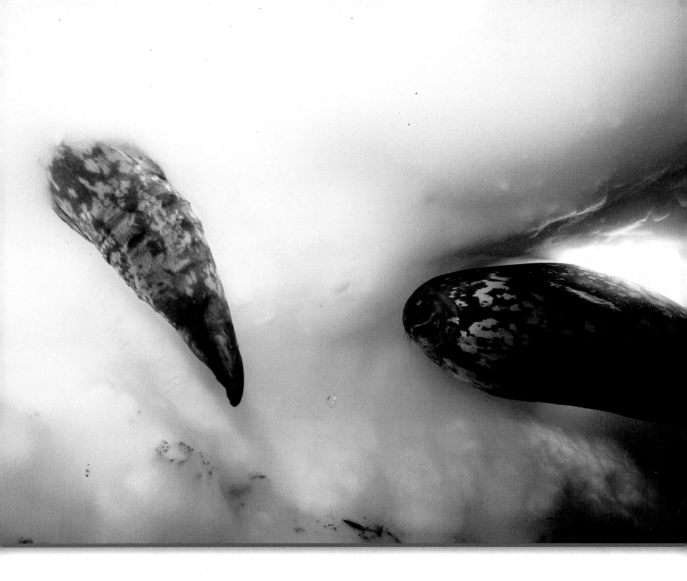

In winter, seals sleep in the water too.

They sleep by holes in the ice so they can breathe when they need to.

# What hunts seals?

In winter, Weddell seals are safe.

Life is too cold and hard in **Antarctica** for other animals that hunt Weddell seals.

In late summer, the ice breaks up for a while.

Killer whales and leopard seals come to hunt Weddell seals.

# Seal body map

back flipper

whiskers

front flipper

# Glossary

 **Antarctica** area around the South Pole

 **blubber** layer of fat around a seal's body that keeps it warm in cold seas

 **breathe** to take air into the body

 **coast** area of land next to the sea

 **flipper** flat part of a seal's body that it uses instead of arms for swimming

 **pup** baby seal

 **whiskers** long, stiff hairs that grow out of an animal's face

# Find out more

## Books

*Seal* (Natural World), Steve Parker (Wayland, 2004)

*Seal* (Wild Britain), Louise and Richard Spilsbury (Heinemann Library, 2004)

## Websites

Watch a video on harp seals and find out about them at: **kids. nationalgeographic.com/Animals/CreatureFeature/Harp-seals**

Listen to the noises different seals make at: **seaworld.org/animal-info/ sound-library/index.htm**

# Index